PARANORMAL
INVESTIGATIONS

Ghosts, Possessions,

and Unexplained Presences

Kate Shoup

Cavendish
Square

New York

Published in 2018 by Cavendish Square Publishing, LLC
243 5th Avenue, Suite 136, New York, NY 10016

Library of Congress Cataloging-in-Publication Data

Names: Shoup, Kate, 1972- author.
Title: Ghosts, possessions, and unexplained presences / Kate Shoup.
Description: New York : Cavendish Square Publishing, 2018. | Series:
Paranormal investigations | Includes bibliographical references and index.
Identifiers: LCCN 2016055207 (print) | LCCN 2016055746 (ebook) |
ISBN 9781502628534 (library bound) | ISBN 9781502628541 (E-book)
Subjects: LCSH: Ghosts. | Occultism. | Spirit possession.
Classification: LCC BF1461 .S47 2018 (print) | LCC BF1461 (ebook) |
DDC 133.1--dc23
LC record available at https://lccn.loc.gov/2016055207

Editorial Director: David McNamara
Editor: Kristen Susienka
Copy Editor: Rebecca Rohan
Associate Art Director: Amy Greenan
Designer: Joseph Macri
Production Coordinator: Karol Szymczuk
Photo Research: J8 Media

Printed in the United States of America

Contents

Bigfoot is just one popular example of people's belief in the paranormal.

The Paranormal

F or thousands of years, people have experienced events they did not understand and could not explain. Sometimes, these were weather patterns, plagues, or natural disasters. Other times, they were something more mysterious—a whispered voice, a sudden slam of the door, or intuition. In response, many developed a belief in the supernatural. According to the *Merriam-Webster Dictionary*, "supernatural" describes something that is "of, relating to, or seeming to come from magic, a god, etc." Indeed, as noted by author and **paranormal** investigator Ben Radford, "All societies have invoked the supernatural to explain things beyond their control and understanding, especially good and bad events." Radford explains, "It's basically the same process as mythology. At one point, people didn't understand why the sun rose and set each day, so they suggested that a chariot pulled the sun across the heavens." Or, "they didn't understand why a child was stillborn, or why a drought occurred, so they came to believe that such events had supernatural causes."

In time, thanks to advances in science, people began to understand many of these strange events. They realized that the sun rose and set because of the way Earth rotated during its journey around the sun. Children were stillborn because of

Some people believe the Hope Diamond is cursed, giving it special powers.

genetic mutations or problems during pregnancy or childbirth (although thanks to advances in medical science, fewer of these occurred each year). Droughts took place because of changes to the climate, ocean temperatures, jet stream, and landscape. But some strange events remained unexplained. These types of unusual events are often described as being paranormal.

Terence Hines, author of *Pseudoscience and the Paranormal*, defines "paranormal" as follows: "The paranormal can best be thought of as a subset of **pseudoscience**. What sets the paranormal apart from other pseudosciences is a reliance on explanations for alleged phenomena that are well outside the bounds of established science." These phenomena, says Hines, "include extrasensory perception (ESP), telekinesis, ghosts, poltergeists, life after death, reincarnation, faith healing, human auras, and so forth." Paranormal also describes such subjects as aliens and unidentified flying objects (UFOs), cursed objects (such as the Hope Diamond), demons, cryptids (animals whose existence remains unproven, such as Bigfoot), and strange places (such as the Bermuda Triangle and Stonehenge).

The Paranormal Investigations series examines many of these paranormal phenomena and delves into the history and the reasons behind each occurrence.

Some people claim to develop paranormal abilities as children.

THE SCIENCE OF PARANORMAL INVESTIGATION

Many people have attempted to learn more about paranormal phenomena using a variety of methods. For example, to learn more about ghosts and demonic **possession**, people often used devices such as Ouija boards to connect with the spirit world.

Modern-day researchers use more high-tech devices to detect fluctuations in electromagnetic fields, ambient temperature, and radiation; sound vibrations; and air quality (which they believe may indicate the presence of a ghost or demon). They also use recording equipment to capture any unusual activity. These techniques have been employed by researchers investigating phenomena such as Bigfoot, the Loch Ness Monster, ghosts, and the Bermuda Triangle.

However, none of these tools meet the scientific "sniff test." That is, there's no proof that any of this equipment actually detects paranormal activity. What it does do is shed light on the possibility of the paranormal and further perpetuate myths of the legends, despite little or no concrete evidence.

Atlantic Ocean

Bermuda

Florida·

Bermuda
triangle

·Puerto Rico

Numerous ships and planes have mysteriously disappeared in the Bermuda Triangle.

Many people believe
in ghosts.

CHAPTER ONE

Ghosts

According to the *Merriam-Webster Dictionary*, a ghost is "the soul of a dead person thought of as living in an unseen world or as appearing to living people." The physical appearance of ghosts is described in different ways. Some people define a ghost as an invisible presence. Others say a ghost is a visible—though sheer or wispy— humanlike form, appearing in death much as they did in life. Regardless of what they're called or what they look like, ghosts are thought to haunt places, people, or things that were significant to them in life.

Some ghosts are believed to be vengeful. Others are seen as kind. Still others are viewed as simply tragic. Ghosts are also said to exhibit different types of behavior. Some make loud noises. Others move or destroy objects. Still others interact with the living—biting, hitting, tripping, or pinching them.

Ghosts Throughout History and Around the World

People all over the world believe in ghosts and have for thousands of years. For example, Sumerians, Babylonians, Assyrians, and members of other Mesopotamian societies believed in ghosts. So, too, did the early Egyptians. Ghosts appear in African, Indian, and Tibetan lore; in Malay and Filipino myths; and Polynesian legend. Ghosts also factor into Thai, Japanese, and Chinese culture. Confucius warned, "Respect ghosts and gods, but keep away from them." Members of one Amazonian rain forest tribe, called the Wari', believe even today that the spirits of dead people, called *jima*, grab the living to wrest their spirits away from them.

As for the ancient Greeks, they didn't just believe in ghosts; they held annual feasts to honor them. According to historian R.C. Finucane, the ancient Greeks invited the ghosts of their ancestors to these feasts, after which these spirits were "firmly invited to leave until the same time next year." Ghosts also appear in ancient Greek literature, including in Homer's *Odyssey* and *Iliad*, and in ancient Greek plays, such as the *Oresteia* by Aeschylus.

Like many other aspects of ancient Greek culture, the notion of ghosts found its way into ancient Rome, too. Chroniclers such as Plutarch and Pliny the Younger wrote of ghosts, as did playwright Plautus and satirist Lucian.

GHOSTS IN THE ARTS

Ghosts frequently appear in books, such as the Charles Dickens classic *A Christmas Carol*; in plays, including *Hamlet* by William Shakespeare; in films, including horror films, dramas such as *Ghost* starring Patrick Swayze and Demi Moore, and comedies, such as *Ghostbusters*; and even children's cartoons, including *Scooby Doo* and *Casper the Friendly Ghost*.

During the Middle Ages, Europeans believed there were two types of ghosts. One type was in fact the soul of a dead person who was stuck in between heaven and hell, in a place called purgatory. These ghosts typically appeared for a specific purpose—for example, to warn the living to confess to their sins, or to make up for the sins they themselves committed. The other type were demons, who existed to either torment or tempt the living. In both cases, the notion of ghosts was closely tied to that of religion (specifically, Catholicism). This explains why people during this period spoke the name of Jesus Christ out loud if they believed they had come across a ghost. If the ghost was the soul of a dead person, the speaker could then find out what it wanted. And if the ghost was a demon, it would be automatically cast out.

GHOSTS AND RELIGION

Many religious texts contain references to ghosts. For example, in the Book of Samuel in the Old Testament of the Christian Bible, the ghost of Samuel appears. Ghosts are also mentioned in the New Testament. One example of this is when Jesus must convince his followers he is not a ghost, as described in the Book of Luke. Another is in discussions about the Holy Ghost, which is part of the Holy Trinity. It's not just Christian religious texts that mention ghosts, however. Islam's holy book, called the Quran, discusses spirits, or jinn.

The belief in ghosts continued into the Renaissance period. The Age of Reason, Reformation, and Counter-Reformation in the sixteenth, seventeenth, and eighteenth centuries, however, brought a backlash against the so-called "dark arts," including the notion of ghosts. By the 1840s, a new movement in both Europe and the United States, called **Spiritualism**, revived people's interest in the subject. According to Spiritualism, the dead lived on in a spirit world. These spirits could communicate with the living through a **medium**, who acted as a go-between.

Interest in the **occult** continues even today. In fact, according to a 2005 Gallup poll, one-third of Americans believe that their "dearly departed" might not be so departed after all. A study by the Associated Press in 2008 showed similar results.

Some people who believe in ghosts suffer from phasmophobia, or the fear of ghosts. These people view ghosts as unnatural at best and evil at worst. Many view a ghost sighting as an **omen** of one's own death. Others who believe in ghosts view these spirits as more kindly. This is especially true for people who live in societies that worship their ancestors, as in many Asian cultures.

The Brown Lady: A Real-Live Ghost?

In December 1835, Lord Charles Townshend invited several friends to his home, Raynham Hall, to celebrate the Christmas holiday. Little did he know that one uninvited guest would also attend. This gate-crasher appeared before two guests, Colonel Loftus and Mr. Hawkins, who spotted her in an upstairs hallway.

Loftus and Hawkins had no idea who this trespasser was. Perhaps more importantly, they had no idea *what* she was. It seemed clear to both men that the woman before them was no living person. For one thing, she appeared to glow. For another, two dark holes appeared where her eyes should have been.

Then there was the woman's outfit: an outdated brown dress. This "Brown Lady," as she became known, was undoubtedly not of this world!

If Loftus and Hawkins had been the only people ever to spot this specter, the story might have died with them. However, a year later, the Brown Lady appeared again—this time to Captain Frederick Marryat. Marryat, doubtful of the claims made by Loftus and Hawkins, had asked to spend the night at Raynham Hall to **debunk** them. During his stay, however, the Brown Lady appeared before him. No one could have been more surprised by this turn of events than Marryat! Indeed, according to his daughter, Florence, he was so startled upon seeing the Brown Lady that he "discharged [his] revolver right in her face." Florence Marryat continued, "The figure instantly disappeared … and the bullet passed through the outer door of the room on the opposite side of the corridor, and lodged in the panel of the inner one."

After the Marryat incident, it would be ninety years before the Brown Lady reappeared—this time revealing herself to a young member of the Townshend family. A decade later, she made her most famous appearance yet. This one, in September 1936, took place before a London-based photographer, Captain Hubert C. Provand, and his assistant, Indre Shira, who were on site to photograph Raynham Hall for *Country Life* magazine. As the professional pair was in the process of shooting the hall's grand staircase, Shira "detected an ethereal, veiled form coming slowly down the stairs." The figure was "transparent so that the steps were visible through the ethereal form," Shire said. "Quick, quick there's something," he cried out to Provand, whose own view of the figure was obscured by the camera's black focusing cloth. Provand took the cap off the camera's lens and Shira triggered

This famous photograph of the Brown Lady of Raynham Hall was captured by Hubert Provand and Indre Shira in 1936.

the flash. Together, they captured what would become an iconic photo of the Brown Lady—one that was published in both *Country Life* and *Time* magazines.

Doubters claimed the photo was a fake, arguing that Provand and Shira had doctored the negative or superimposed one photo over another. But an independent witness who was present when they developed the original negative confirmed this was not the case. There have been few—if any—sightings of the Brown Lady since that incident. Nevertheless, to this day she remains a source of great curiosity, each year drawing countless visitors to Raynham Hall, which is now open to the public.

Who Was the Brown Lady?

Most people believe the Brown Lady is the ghost of Lady Dorothy Walpole. In 1713, Lady Dorothy married Charles Townshend and moved to his family home, Raynham Hall. A statesman who had won the favor of King George I (though was merely tolerated by his successor, King George II), Townshend was a colleague of Lady Dorothy's elder brother Robert Walpole, who himself became prime minister of Great Britain in 1721.

According to local records, Lady Dorothy died in 1726. But did she *really*? Rumor had it that Lady Dorothy had had an affair with a man named Lord Wharton, a known ne'er-do-well. Some believe that when the famously ill-tempered Townshend learned of this betrayal, he held a mock funeral for his wife, who remained very much alive. He then locked her away in Raynham Hall, where she remained until her actual death some years later.

The Brown Lady is said to be the ghost of Lady Dorothy Townshend.

Other Ghosts (and Where to Find Them)

The Brown Lady of Raynham Hall is just one example of a ghost sighting. There have been countless others all over the world, dating back hundreds or even thousands of years. To quote British author Charles Dickens (who was, coincidentally, friendly with Captain Frederick Marryat), "There is no end to the old houses with resounding galleries, and dismal state-bedchambers, and haunted wings shut up for many years, through which we may ramble, with an agreeable creeping up our back, and encounter any number of ghosts."

Rambling country houses aren't the only stomping grounds for ghosts, however. Some people claim they've seen ghosts in prisons. Employees at Alcatraz, which served as a US federal prison from 1934 to 1963, have reported hearing strange clanging sounds, banjo music, men's voices, and even screams. And many believe that one cell, 14D, is haunted. "There's a feeling of sudden intensity that comes from spending more than a few minutes around that cell," said one guard. Another former prison, the Tower of London, is said to be haunted. There, guards and visitors claim to have spotted the ghosts of Thomas A. Becket, Lady Arbella Stuart, and Queen Anne Boleyn. Also sighted: the so-called "young princes," Edward V and his brother Richard, who historians believe were murdered in the tower by their double-crossing uncle, the Duke of Gloucester. Hospitals, asylums, and theaters are other common locations for ghost sightings.

Some people even believe they've seen ghosts in the White House. It's said that the ghost of First Lady Dolley Madison protects the famous Rose Garden; First Lady Abigail Adams hangs laundry in the East Room; and President Thomas

Ghosts are rumored to haunt the halls of Alcatraz.

Jefferson plays his violin in the Yellow Oval Room. The ghost of President John Tyler haunts the Blue Room, President Andrew Jackson the Queen's Bedroom, and President William Henry Harrison the attic. And famous people ranging from First Lady Grace Coolidge, British prime minister Winston Churchill, and Queen Wilhelmina of the Netherlands claim they've spied the ghost of President Abraham Lincoln.

HOAX: BORLEY RECTORY

Some reports of ghost sightings are false, or **hoaxes**. One famous hoax took place in a mansion in England called Borley Rectory. Residents claimed the mansion was haunted. They said they had heard mysterious bells ringing and had seen windows shatter for no apparent reason. A paranormal researcher, Harry Price, backed up these claims. He described Borley Rectory as "the most haunted house in England." After Price's death in 1948, however, members of the Society for Psychical Research (SPR) concluded that the story was a hoax.

These days, thanks to computer software like Photoshop, it's easy to carry out a ghost-related hoax—especially when photographs are involved. There are even apps for smartphones that enable people to quickly add ghost-like auras to their digital photographs.

Borley Rectory was the site of a well-known hoax.

Some people use a Ouija board to try to connect with spirits.

CHAPTER TWO

Spiritualism Explored ... and Debunked?

Some people are afraid of ghosts and want to stay as far away from them as possible. Others, driven by their curiosity, seek to find ghosts, learn more about them, and even communicate with them.

Mediums in the Age of Spiritualism

This was especially true during the nineteenth century, when both the United States and Great Britain saw a rise in Spiritualism. Spiritualism was the belief that dead people lived on in a kind of spirit world. Not surprisingly, there was also a rise in mediums during this time. A medium is someone who claims to bridge the divide between the living and the dead, enabling them to communicate.

Some mediums said they could "tune in" to the spirit world. They claimed that this practice—sometimes called mental mediumship—enabled them to speak to and relay messages from dead people. Other mediums were said to **channel** spirits. In other words, they allowed spirits to "borrow" their body and use it to communicate by speaking, writing, drawing, or tapping. Some mediums communicated with spirits during a special session called a **séance**. A séance,

SPIRIT PHOTOGRAPHY

As interest in Spiritualism grew, so too did the practice of spirit photography—that is, attempting to capture photographic images of ghosts. The first spirit photographer was William H. Mumler. After discovering a ghost-like image in one of his own photographs, Mumler became a medium, photographing his participants during each session. Mumler was eventually found to be a fraud, however. He simply doctored his negatives to add the image of the dearly departed to the photo. So, too, were other so-called spirit photographers.

Spirit photographers claimed to capture images of ghosts.

According to Harry Price, the famous ghost hunter who in addition to studying events at Borley Rectory also investigated the case of the Brown Lady photo taken by Provand and Shira at Raynham Hall, "There is *no* good evidence that a spirit photograph has ever been produced." That's not to say no spirit had ever been caught on film, however. Even Price believed the photograph of the Brown Lady was authentic. The difference? Price believed the photographers who captured *her* image had no secret motives.

typically held in a darkened room, was also attended by the loved ones of the deceased.

Some mediums used special tools to communicate with the dead. One was a Ouija board, also called a talking board or a spirit board. A Ouija board is a flat board with the letters of the alphabet; the numbers zero through nine; the words "yes," "no," and sometimes "goodbye"; and certain symbols. To use a Ouija board, the medium and participants placed their fingers on a small, heart-shaped object, sometimes called a planchette, which rested on the board. The medium then posed questions to the spirit with which the group wanted to communicate. To answer the questions, the spirit would cause the planchette to move about the board, pointing at the various letters, numbers, words, or symbols to spell out their message.

"Scientific" Societies

In 1882, the Society for Psychical Research (SPR) formed in Great Britain. (Its American counterpart, the American Society for Psychical Research—ASPR for short—formed three years later.) The purpose of the SPR was "to approach [Spiritualism] without prejudice or prepossession of any kind, and in the same spirit of exact and unimpassioned enquiry which has enabled science to solve so many problems, once not less obscure nor less hotly debated."

Members of the SPR, ASPR, and other similar groups probed paranormal claims. Sometimes, they confirmed the claim, as Price did at Raynham Hall. Other times, they debunked it. This happened with Nandor Fodor, who investigated the Thornton Heath case of 1938. In this case, a woman named Mrs. Forbes claimed to be hounded by a poltergeist. But Fodor quickly determined that the "poltergeist" was in fact Mrs. Forbes herself. (Later, after years of research, Fodor would conclude that a "poltergeist is not a ghost. It is a bundle of projected repressions.") As noted by author Rosemary Guiley, "Fodor asserted that the psychosis was an episodic mental disturbance of schizophrenic character," noting that "Mrs. Forbes's unconscious mind was responsible for the activities finally determined to be fraudulent."

Friend or Fraud?

It's no surprise that many people longed to be able to contact loved ones who had died. Unfortunately, this longing made them easy targets for scammers. All too often, people with no actual Spiritualist abilities posed as mediums to trick these vulnerable folks into paying hefty fees to communicate with their dearly departed. Indeed, it's believed that most (if not all) mediums during the Spiritualist era, which reached its peak between the 1840s and the 1920s, were fakes.

Medium William Stainton Moses worked in the late 1800s.

These frauds used a variety of techniques to fool their customers. One was to simply alter their vocal pattern or behavior when "channeling" the dead. Anyone with even a small measure of theatrical talent could manage this easily. Or, if using a Ouija board, the medium—not the deceased—would move the planchette to spell out a message. And merely by using the power of suggestion within a darkened room, these swindlers could often convince their audience that a spirit was present.

To appear more convincing, many of these fakes researched their customers

HEREWARD CARRINGTON

One famous debunker was Hereward Carrington. Born in Great Britain in 1880, Carrington moved to America at the age of eight. In 1907, he joined the ASPR. He quickly gained a reputation as a clever investigator of psychic phenomena. Carrington exposed several fraudulent mediums and their tricks. Later, Carrington—who would go on to write nearly one hundred books on a variety of topics, including the paranormal—claimed that "there may be much fraud in modern Spiritualism, in fact, I am disposed to believe that fully 98 percent of the phenomena, both mental and physical, are fraudulently produced." However, Carrington was unwilling to debunk Spiritualism completely. He believed that "there must have been some genuine phenomena at the commencement of this movement, in order that the first mediums may have copied them by fraudulent means, and that a certain percentage of the phenomena occurring to-day is genuine."

ahead of time. Sometimes, they found articles about them in the newspaper. Or they simply spied on their conversations when they arrived for the séance. Some used a technique called cold reading to obtain information about their mark. That is, they studied the person's age, gender, ethnicity, manner of speech, place of origin, education, religion, clothing and jewelry, and hairstyle for clues about their situation and personality.

Some so-called "mediums" went even farther, using costumes or props to trick their audience. Others used sleight-of-hand techniques common among stage magicians. Indeed, magicians—including the famous Harry Houdini— were responsible for exposing several fraudulent mediums.

Ghost Hunting Today

As noted in *Encyclopedia Britannica*, "the exposure of widespread fraud within the Spiritualist movement severely damaged its reputation." Nevertheless, many people still believe in ghosts and continue to investigate claims of paranormal activity. These people call themselves ghost hunters.

In addition to the old-fashioned methods already discussed, modern-day ghost hunters use numerous types of high-tech equipment in their efforts to identify paranormal activity. Most of these devices are designed to detect changes in the environment. One such device is an electromagnetic field detector, which senses disruptions to electromagnetic fields. Another is a Geiger counter, which ghost hunters use to detect radiation. In addition to these, modern-day ghost hunters use thermographic or infrared video to detect deviations in the ambient temperature and special audio recorders to capture sounds that are inaudible to humans.

Modern-day ghost hunters use high-tech equipment.

Not everyone is convinced that these tools are effective, however. That is, while they may indeed detect changes in the environment, there's no proof that those changes indicate the presence of a ghost. As noted by author Benjamin Radford, who has studied the practices of these modern-day ghost hunters, "The supposed links between ghosts and electromagnetic fields, low temperatures, radiation, odd photographic images, and so on are based on nothing more than guesses, unproven theories, and wild conjecture." For example, deviations in electromagnetic fields are more likely caused by the presence of electrical wires and devices (including those carried by the ghost hunters themselves) than by a ghost. Similarly, the presence of radiation is explained by the presence of decaying subatomic particles, *not* a ghost. (As noted by one **skeptic**, Robert Todd Carroll, "Unless ghosts are made of atoms they are not emitting subatomic particles.") Changes in ambient temperature, detected by the use of special video-capture devices, are almost certainly caused by real, live people or animals. And mysterious noises captured by special audio-recording devices, sometimes called electronic voice phenomena (EVP), could be, well, just about anything.

The fact is, says Radford, "If a device could reliably determine the presence or absence of ghosts, then by definition, ghosts would be proven to exist." Even a cursory investigation of these techniques will quickly reveal "to anyone with a background in science that the methods used are both illogical and unscientific," says Radford. This is unfortunate because, as noted by Radford, "I believe that if ghosts exist, they are important and deserve to be taken seriously. Most of the efforts to investigate ghosts so far have been badly flawed and unscientific—and not surprisingly, fruitless."

People are said to be "possessed" when their body is taken over by a demon, devil, or evil spirit.

Possession

Possession occurs when a demon, devil, or evil spirit takes control of a living person's body. Someone who is possessed is called a **demoniac**. Often, demoniacs act very agitated and exhibit many strange behaviors. For example, a demoniac may become foul-mouthed. Their voice, manner of speaking, or even their personality may change. Some demoniacs experience xenoglossy, or the sudden ability to speak a foreign language. Others gain obscure knowledge that was previously unknown to them—a condition called gnosis. Still others experience glossolalia, or speaking in tongues. There are also many physical signs. These may include fits, fainting, or contortions, or the demoniac's facial structure might change. Sometimes, the demoniac suffers mysterious injuries, such as bites, scratch marks, or lesions. Some demoniacs gain superhuman strength. And many demoniacs demonstrate an aversion to sacred objects, such as relics or crosses.

Possession is different from channeling. Channeling is when someone permits a spirit to enter their body. With channeling, the person remains in control of their body and can cast out the spirit at any time. With possession, the demoniac remains possessed until the spirit chooses or is forced to leave their body.

Some view victims of possession as blameless. They have no control over their actions. Others insist that the victim holds some blame. Malachi Martin, author of *Hostage to the Devil*, writes, "no person can be possessed without some degree of cooperation on his or her part."

SYMPTOMS OF POSSESSION

During the 1600s, Roman Catholic Church officials teamed up to identify the symptoms of possession so they could diagnose the condition. This meeting, which took place in the French town of Louviers, followed an incident in a local convent in which nuns were believed to be possessed. They identified several symptoms: leading a wicked life, living outside the rules of society, saying curse words, behaving violently, having a frightening facial expression, making animal sounds or movements, and taking off one's clothes in public. Other symptoms included saying curse words while prayers were spoken, seeming afraid of sacred objects, being plagued by spirits, believing one to be possessed, and being unable to remember fits after they took place. Finally, they listed such symptoms as being sick for a long time, sleeping too deeply, vomiting strange objects (such as toads, maggots, or nails), and feeling tired of living.

Possession Throughout History and Around the World

The notion of possession is not new, nor is it limited to just one part of the world. Scholars believe the Sumerians first conceived of possession. They believed that "sickness demons" possessed the body and caused disease. They also prayed to certain gods to protect themselves from these demons or cast them out of their body. Certain **shamanic** cultures shared similar beliefs, blaming disease on evil spirits. And the Gurage people in Ethiopia have long thought that certain illnesses are caused by an evil spirit.

In general, possession by evil spirits is a religious concept. This is particularly true for Christianity. The Old Testament contains several references to possession. One is the "evil spirit from the Lord [that] troubled" Saul but departed when David played the harp. Another is the "lying spirit [that] entered the mouths of false prophets." The Old Testament also offers pointers for casting out these demons, noting that "if a devil or an evil spirit trouble any, we must make a smoke thereof before the man or the woman, and the party shall be no more

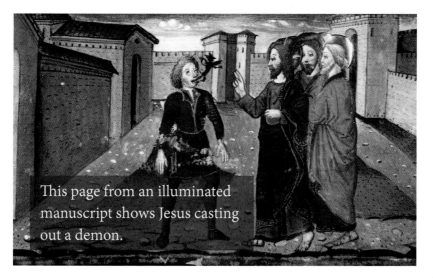

This page from an illuminated manuscript shows Jesus casting out a demon.

vexed." The New Testament contains even more references to possession. Most of these are stories about Jesus casting out demons from the body of a possessed person. This takes place in the books of Matthew, Mark, Luke, and John. Demons also appear in several verses of Acts and in Revelations. These demons were believed to be fallen angels—that is, wicked or rebellious angels that were cast out of heaven.

Antoine Gay: Possessed by a Demon?

As a young man, a Frenchman named Antoine Gay dreamed of becoming a monk. Finally, in 1836, he achieved his dream. After a career as a soldier and later as a carpenter, Gay joined the brotherhood of monks at the Abbaye Notre-Dame d'Aiguebelle. He was forty-six years old.

Just one year later, Gay left the abbey. Doctors and church officials cited a "nervous disorder" as the reason for his departure. However, they soon became convinced something more sinister was afoot: Gay was possessed by a demon. One church official, Father Burnoud, wrote to the Bishop of Grenoble: "We consider it very probable that this man is possessed by a devil." To support this claim, Father Burnoud offered several pieces of evidence. First, Gay had "disclosed several secret things which he had no means of knowing." Second, "there were visible signs of discontent when we pronounced various formulae and prayers of the ritual in Latin." This was significant because "Gay does not know Latin." Father Burnoud believed "we can only attribute these contortions ... to the presence of a higher intelligence." Further, "we questioned [Gay] several times in Latin and since the replies were made in French through the mouth of Master Gay, this seems to indicate a knowledge of Latin on the part

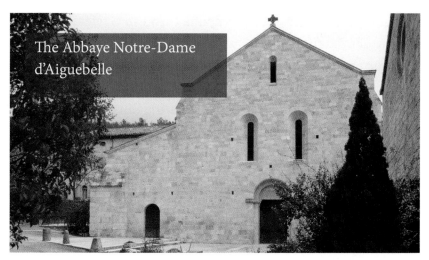

The Abbaye Notre-Dame d'Aiguebelle

of that higher intelligence." Finally, Father Burnoud claimed that numerous testimonials by "worthy and reliable persons" vouched for Gay's good faith, virtue, and sincerity. That meant, said Father Burnoud, that "Gay is not playing tricks: in that case, he must be possessed."

After examining Gay, a physician named Dr. Pictet agreed with Father Burnoud. In 1843, Pictet wrote that "we have not been able to discover the least sign of moral or physical weakness." The doctor concluded, "[Gay's] extraordinary state can only be attributed to possession." This conviction was reinforced by the fact that "during our first interview with M. Gay, that extraordinary thing which speaks through his mouth revealed the inmost secrets of our heart, told us the story of our life from the age of twelve onwards, giving details that are known only to God, our confessor, and ourselves."

Officials determined that the demon was named Isacaron. It had possessed Gay some ten years earlier. This was done under orders from God himself, to instruct humans on Christ, God, the Holy Spirit, and the Virgin Mother. "It is heaven's will, which all must obey, that I, the devil Isacaron, possessing the body of Gay, should speak through his mouth,"

Isacaron said. When Isacaron spoke through Gay, writes author Leon Cristiani, "[Gay's] voice would change, becoming raucous and producing an outburst of shouting, laden with insults and abuse. The man who had previously been all gentleness and humility suddenly became bitter, sarcastic and foul-mouthed."

Isacaron did more than just speak through Gay. He also caused various physical symptoms in the man, such as foaming at the mouth, contorting his body, throwing himself to the ground, and performing acrobatic movements. An incident in 1850 revealed an even stranger behavior: Gay met a young woman named Chiquette, who was also possessed. Her demon's name was Madeste. Gay and Chiquette had never met each other, but according to one witness, Father Chiron, "the devils in possession knew each other well." Indeed, said Father Chiron, "No sooner had [Madeste] encountered the presence of Isacaron than a remarkably violent dialogue arose between the two fallen angels." They "sounded like mad dogs. They spoke a totally unknown language, very softly and we understood nothing. I was later informed by Isacaron, who translated the dispute for me, that it was on a question of precedence, as to which was the greater of the two. They insulted and poured scorn on each other. I was often obliged to stand between them to prevent their coming to blows." This behavior, in the view of Father Chiron, was "inexplicable except as cases of possession."

Unfortunately, Gay was never freed from his tormentor. Cristiani posits that this was because the demon Isacaron was "obeying God's orders" by possessing Gay. Interestingly, Isacaron seemed as unhappy about this state of affairs as Gay. According to Cristiani, "There is abundant proof that Isacaron wished to be relieved of his task ... so that he could depart." Once, after spotting a priest nearby, Isacaron called out through

Gay, "That is a man! That is a priest! You shall tell him to say a mass for the deliverance of the possessed, and to have my power over his body removed before his deliverance." Sadly, neither Gay nor Isacaron would be relieved of their shared burden. Gay continued to display signs of possession until his death in 1871 at the age of eighty-one. In all, he had been host to Isacaron for more than forty years.

Other Tales of Possession

Antoine Gay is just one tale of possession. There are many others. One was the case of Madeleine de Demandolx de la Palud, a nineteen-year-old nun in Aix-en-Provence, France. In 1611, this young nun displayed what was believed to be signs of demonic possession. These signs included destroying a crucifix in a fit of rage. She was one of eight nuns believed to be afflicted. A similar event took place in a convent in Loudun, France, in 1634, and again in a convent in Louviers, France, in 1647. (It was this event that spurred Roman Catholic Church officials to identify the symptoms of possession.)

In 1618, church officials diagnosed another Frenchwoman, Elizabeth de Ranfaing, with diabolical possession. During her treatment, which lasted several years, the demon inside her allegedly spoke to church officials in varying languages, including French, Greek, Latin, Hebrew, and Italian. This demon was also said to recite both the thoughts and the sins of the young woman's examiners. Finally, the demon demonstrated considerable knowledge of the rites of the Catholic Church. During one treatment session, when the exorcist flubbed his recital of a church rite, the demon quickly cut in to correct him. Ultimately, de Ranfaing's treatment proved unsuccessful. However, after she took a series of pilgrimages starting in April 1826, her symptoms disappeared.

Yet another tale of possession came from the Massachusetts Bay Colony. This involved a woman named Dorothy Talbye. According to Governor John Winthrop, in his *History of New England*, Talbye suffered from "melancholy or spiritual delusions." Winthrop believed this explained why, in 1638, Talbye "was so possessed with Satan that he persuaded her … to break the neck of her own child that she might free it from future misery." She was hanged for this crime.

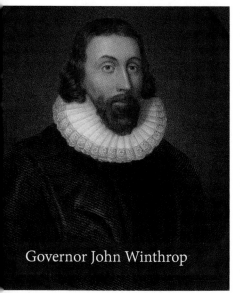

Governor John Winthrop

Then there was Elizabeth Knapp, also in the Massachusetts Bay Colony. Knapp, a sixteen-year-old servant in the home of Reverend Samuel Willard, first complained of pains throughout her body. Then she experienced emotional fits, characterized by convulsions, hysterics, and weeping fits. She was plagued by hallucinations. She became violent, and it took three or even four people to restrain her. Sometimes, she spoke in a deep voice or made animal sounds. Once, she attempted to throw herself into the fire. No medical doctor could diagnose her. This left Willard to conclude that she was possessed—a conclusion that Knapp herself confirmed. No one knows what happened to Knapp, including whether she was ever freed from her demon.

THE CASE OF ROBBIE MANNHEIM

In 1949, newspapers reported the possession of a teenaged boy they called Robbie Mannheim (not his real name). These accounts claimed that when Robbie was nearby, his family heard strange noises and saw furniture and other objects move unaided. Also, the boy's voice changed, and it seemed he could suddenly speak Latin. Finally, several marks appeared on the boy's body.

Later research showed that this case was likely a hoax. Author Mark Opsasnick interviewed several of the boy's neighbors and childhood friends and concluded that "the boy had been a very clever trickster, who had pulled pranks to frighten his mother and to fool children in the neighborhood." Famed skeptic Joe Nickell agreed, noting that there was "simply no credible evidence to suggest the boy was possessed by demons or evil spirits," and that "nothing that was reliably reported in the case was beyond the abilities of a teenager to produce." Still, the tale of Robbie Mannheim served as the inspiration for the classic horror movie *The Exorcist*.

A scene from the famous horror movie *The Exorcist*

Church officials use a rite called
exorcism to treat people they
believe are possessed.

CHAPTER FOUR

Exorcism

C hurch officials use a technique called **exorcism** to treat people who they believe are possessed. The term stems from the Greek word *exousia*, which means "oath." Scholar James R. Lewis explains, "To exorcise thus means something along the lines of placing the possessing spirit under oath—invoking a higher authority to compel the spirit—rather than an actual 'casting out.'"

Exorcism is particularly prevalent within the Roman Catholic Church. Indeed, Roman Catholic priests from all over the world travel to the Vatican, where top church officials are headquartered, to be trained in exorcism. These priests are called exorcists. There are more than fifty Vatican-trained exorcists in the United States alone. Other self-declared exorcists exist, but most of these are probably fakes.

Understanding Exorcisms

To determine whether an exorcism is needed, exorcists follow a multistep process. First, they subject the alleged demoniac to both a psychiatric and physical evaluation. Next, they attempt to identify how the demon might have entered that person. They believe engaging in black magic, worshipping the occult, or even just playing with a Ouija board is enough to engage a demon. The exorcist then looks for signs of demonic possession. For example, they see whether the person engages in xenoglossy, gnosis, or glossolalia. They also look for physical signs, such as fits, fainting, contortions, changes to the person's facial structure, or mysterious injuries, as well as superhuman strength. Finally, they determine whether the person demonstrates an aversion to sacred objects. If the result of this investigation points to possession, then the exorcist seeks permission from church leaders to proceed with the exorcism.

Before commencing with an exorcism, the exorcist must undergo a purifying process. As explained by one exorcist, the Most Reverend Dr. Isaac Kramer, "We actually have to spend days celebrating the mass, going to confessions—spiritually cleansing and purging ourselves of all our sins." Otherwise, says Kramer, it's "something the demon can use against the priest to overwhelm them." Or, he says, "the demons technically could ignore me, if I didn't go through the purification process."

An exorcism involves several rituals. First, according to Father Gary Thomas, who is also an exorcist, "There's a set of prayers that we pray right before the exorcism starts." These prayers, he explains, "establish God's authority, protect the team, protect the person that's the subject of the exorcism, and protect the property on which the exorcism is taking place." Next, says Father Thomas, "you anoint the doors with blessed oil so the demon cannot leave." Then the exorcist performs the rite. "It's done entirely in Latin," Father Thomas explains. "You begin with the litany of the saints, followed by scripture, followed by a few words based on the scriptures, and then you address prayers to God, and address prayers to Satan. In between, you can pray the Hail Mary and the Lord's Prayer." Sometimes, the exorcist waves a charm or icon to attempt to drive out the demon. This continues until the demon—or, more commonly, demons, plural—leaves. Often, several exorcisms, over a period of days, weeks, months, or even years, may be required to achieve that aim. Even then, the person must be careful to avoid behaviors that may allow the demon back in, such as dabbling in the occult.

For the demoniac, an exorcism can be a profoundly unpleasant experience—though perhaps not as painful as it is often depicted in movies. "It never gets to the point where someone's head spins and they puke pea soup, like Hollywood likes to show," says Reverend Kramer. Still, attempts to coax the demon from the body often cause the victim to scream in pain. Many must be restrained.

A priest performs an exorcism on a man believed to be possessed.

Interestingly, exorcisms aren't performed just for cases of possession. They're also performed in response to three other types of demonic activity: vexation, obsession, and infestation. Vexation is when a demon physically attacks its victim, leaving cuts, scrapes, burns, and bruises. These are by far the most common form of demonic activity. According to famed exorcist Father Gabriele Amorth, vexations are believed to be caused by "a person's cultivation of imprudent habits, by frequenting wizards or séances, through repeated and serious sins, or by submitting to spells." Obsession is when a demon violates its victim mentally, triggering persistent thoughts of evil. "In these cases," says Father Amorth, "the person is no longer master of his own thoughts." Finally, infestation is when a demon invades an object, an animal, or a place. This, says Father Amorth, "provokes great sufferings and, at times, enormous economic damage to the property and to the one subjected to it."

This house inspired the movie *The Exorcist*.

REAL, FAKE, OR MENTAL ILLNESS?

Many behaviors attributed to possession may instead be—indeed, almost certainly *are*—the result of a physical or mental illness. Examples of such illnesses include hysteria, mania, psychosis, Tourette's syndrome, epilepsy, schizophrenia, and dissociative identity disorder. For proof, famed skeptic Joe Nickell cites the fact that "as mental illness began to be recognized as such after the seventeenth century, there was a consequent decline in demonic superstitions." Indeed, in 1999, the Vatican updated its guidelines for casting out demons, "urging exorcists to avoid mistaking psychiatric illness for possession."

Mental illness isn't the only possible explanation for this type of behavior, however. According to Nickell, "Possession was sometimes feigned by nuns to act out sexual frustrations, protest restrictions, escape unpleasant duties, attract attention and sympathy, and fulfill other useful functions." To support this claim, Nickell rightfully reminds his audience that "possession can be childishly simple to fake."

Famous Exorcisms

There have been several famous exorcisms. One is the exorcism of Englishman Michael Taylor. In 1974, several church officials attempted an exorcism to cast out the numerous demons believed to possess him. According to Bill Ellis, author of *Raising the Devil: Satanism, New Religions, and the Media*, "In an all-night ceremony, the group invoked and cast out at least forty demons, including those of incest, bestiality, blasphemy, and lewdness. At the end, exhausted, they allowed Taylor to go home, although they felt that at least three demons—insanity, murder, and violence—were still left in him." Based on what Taylor did next, it appears these clergymen were correct. Later that night, Taylor brutally murdered his wife and their dog. (He was acquitted on the grounds of insanity, though required to undergo psychiatric treatment.)

In another case, also during the 1970s, twenty-year-old Anneliese Michel of Germany began hearing voices and showed increasing intolerance of religious objects. She soon became convinced she was possessed by demons. Church officials agreed and intervened in an attempt to treat her.

Over a period of ten months, Michel endured sixty-seven exorcism sessions, each lasting as many as four hours. Unfortunately, however, Michel's demons (who priests said included Lucifer, Cain, Judas Iscariot, Hitler, and Nero) remained. Demoralized, Michel—whose near-constant kneeling in a prayer position had resulted in two broken knees—stopped eating. Malnourished and dehydrated, she quickly withered to a mere 68 pounds (30 kilograms). On July 1, 1976, she died of starvation.

A memorial to Anneliese Michel, who died due to an exorcism

Michel's exorcists claimed she had been freed of her demons before her death. Nevertheless, they, along with the young woman's parents, were tried and convicted of negligent manslaughter.

A SOMETIMES DEADLY PRACTICE

Anneliese Michel is not the only person to die due to an exorcism. In 2003, the congregation of a church in Milwaukee, Wisconsin, attempted to "cure" eight-year-old Torrance Cantrell of his autism. They bound him up in sheets to keep him from scratching himself, held him down, and prayed for more than an hour. "We were asking God to take this spirit that was tormenting this little boy to death," recalled one witness. Sadly, the boy suffocated and died.

A similar tragedy took place in 2005. In that case, a young nun named Maricica Irina Cornici was brought to a convent after suffering what a psychiatrist believed were symptoms of schizophrenia. The convent's priest thought she was possessed and attempted an exorcism. He tied the young woman to a cross, gagged her, and left her for three days without food or water. There, she died of suffocation and dehydration.

Charles Fort, a paranormal
researcher, circa 1920

CHAPTER FIVE

Searching for Meaning

I t's one thing for someone to claim to have experienced or witnessed a paranormal event, such as a ghost sighting or possession. It's quite another for them to *prove* the event took place. There are a couple of key reasons for this.

Researching the Paranormal

First, few paranormal events leave no physical evidence, making it difficult to confirm the event took place. Most evidence of paranormal activity is anecdotal in nature. That is, the evidence consists of stories told by those who claim to have experienced a paranormal event of some kind. This is problematic because its accuracy rests solely on the credibility of the person relaying the story.

Second, by their very definition, paranormal phenomena do not adhere to the laws of nature. Therefore, it is impossible to evaluate claims of a paranormal event using the scientific method. *Merriam-Webster Dictionary* defines the scientific method as "principles and procedures for the systematic pursuit of knowledge involving the recognition and formulation of a problem, the collection of data though observation and experiment, and the formulation and testing of hypotheses." This leaves traditional scientists with no reliable method by which to evaluate claims of the paranormal.

Still, researchers continue to study the paranormal. This field of study is commonly referred to as **parapsychology**. Some researchers focus on simply collecting anecdotal evidence of paranormal events. One researcher named Charles Fort collected as many as forty thousand anecdotes about paranormal events from news clippings and other journalistic sources. These anecdotes ranged in topic from poltergeist events to stories of levitation, mysterious appearances and disappearances, and more. Using these sources, Fort published four nonfiction books about the paranormal. Many consider him to be the "father of modern paranormalism." Indeed, his name eventually morphed into an adjective to describe paranormal events: *Fortean.*

Other researchers take a participant-observer approach. These individuals immerse themselves in the subject of the paranormal in the hopes of gaining a better understanding of it. (This is the approach favored by the modern-day ghost hunters described in chapter 2.) They make special attempts to observe and experience paranormal phenomena, but focus less on explaining those phenomena. This method is problematic, however. One problem with this approach is subjectivity, or bias. As noted by Professor Barbara A. Sommer, "Events are interpreted through the single observer's eyes … Clearly one's own views can come into play." Another problem with this approach is reactivity—that is, influencing what you're observing. Finally, there's no systematic way to gather data using this technique. As a result, the data that *is* gathered is less reliable.

WHY DO WE BELIEVE?

More than one-third of Americans believe in ghosts. Even more believe in demonic possession. If scientific research has failed to prove that paranormal events are real, why do so many people believe in them? Author Robert L. Park suggests one simple reason: "A lot of people want it to be so." Some researchers suggest that people who believe they've experienced a paranormal event have, in fact, been fooled by their own brains. Others are less generous, offering hypotheses that include ignorance, deprivation, and deficiency. Author Dean Radin explains, "The ignorance hypothesis asserts that people believe in the paranormal because they're uneducated or stupid. The deprivation hypothesis proposes that these beliefs exist to provide a way to cope in the face of psychological uncertainties and physical stressors. The deficiency hypothesis asserts that such beliefs arise because people are mentally defective in some way, ranging from low intelligence or poor critical thinking ability to full-blown psychosis."

While it's true that no one has definitively proved ghosts and demons (and other paranormal phenomena) exist, it's also true that no one has definitively proved they *don't* exist. However, to quote television personality Mike Rowe, "We need to stop confusing the inability to prove that ghosts do not exist as evidence that they might." Rowe continues, "The burden of proof has shifted to the point that skepticism … is now dismissed as cynicism, and those who doubt the existence of [the paranormal] are often labeled as 'close-minded.'"

SKEPTICS

Some researchers tackle the subject of parapsychology from the position of a skeptic. Many of these skeptical researchers belong to an organization called the Committee for Skeptical Inquiry (CSI), founded by Carl Sagan, Isaac Asimov, and others. According to its website, CSI "encourages the critical investigation of controversial or extraordinary claims from a responsible, scientific point of view and disseminates factual information about the results of such inquiries to the scientific community, the media, and the public." Members of this organization generally believe that parapsychology is in fact a pseudoscience, and that so-called "paranormal events" are simply natural phenomena that are misinterpreted, misunderstood, out of the ordinary, or the result of fraudulent activity. CSI members are so convinced of this, one member, James Randi, even offered a $1 million prize to anyone who proved to possess paranormal or supernatural abilities. Despite thousands of attempts over the course of nearly two decades to claim the prize, no one ever has.

One might reasonably conclude that only crackpots and crazies research the paranormal, but that's not the case. Several highly regarded universities offer studies in the paranormal. For example, the Koestler Parapsychology Unit at the University of Edinburgh, which is part of the university's psychology department, studies out-of-the-ordinary experiences and belief in the paranormal. It also maintains a library of materials on the topic. A similar program exists at the University of Virginia, called the Division of Perceptual Studies (DOPS). Its mission is to normalize the notion that "the scientific empirical investigation of phenomena that suggest that currently accepted scientific assumptions and theories about the nature of mind or consciousness, and its relation to matter, may be incomplete." The University of California Los Angeles once boasted a similar lab, the Neuropsychiatric Institute (NPI). According to journalist Jake Flanagin, it "conducted scientific experiments in clairvoyance, telepathy, and haunted houses." Kerry Gaynor, who served as a research assistant at the lab, recalled, "We were getting calls and letters every day. We were hearing about this kind of phenomena from all around the country and all around the world." However, the university closed the lab in 1978.

The Media's Impact

Often, the mass media—movies, TV shows, books, and even news stories—reinforces people's belief in the paranormal. For example, paranormal activity is a popular subject in film. It even has its own genre: horror. Classic horror films include *The Exorcist* (based on the Robbie Mannheim case), *Poltergeist*, *The Shining*, *The Omen*, and others.

The paranormal is also a common topic on TV. Even networks like the Discovery Channel and A&E, which were originally launched to provide educational programming, air shows about the paranormal. And daytime talk shows often feature guests who claim they've experienced a paranormal event.

Indeed, an entire industry has grown around the subject of the paranormal—and that industry might not care much about conveying factual information. As noted by psychologist Richard Wiseman, "The books, the television shows … all have a vested interest in getting the public to believe this stuff."

Unfortunately, there is little in the way of critical coverage in the media to serve as a counterweight. Professor Paul Kurtz points out, "In regard to the many talk shows that constantly deal with paranormal topics, the skeptical viewpoint is rarely heard; and when it is permitted to be expressed, it is usually sandbagged by the host or other guests." This likely influences people to believe in paranormal phenomena, even if they may not exist.

Evolving Theories

Science is an evolving field. Every day, new information prompts scientists to reevaluate what they know and adjust their understanding of the world accordingly. This could happen with regard to paranormal events. For example, scientists might develop some new technology that enables them to detect the presence of ghosts or demons. Or perhaps they'll come up with a new way to validate the existence of these paranormal phenomena. Or maybe some large-scale paranormal event with many witnesses will take place, making it impossible to deny its occurrence.

Some day, new information could reveal that people who experience paranormal events aren't ignorant, deprived, or deficient; they're *right*. But unless and until that happens, it's wise to remain skeptical. That doesn't mean one can't be open-minded on the topic of the paranormal. In the words of the famous psychiatrist Carl Jung, "I shall not commit the fashionable stupidity of regarding everything I cannot explain as a fraud." But it does mean that one should take any claims of paranormal activity with a grain of salt.

SMILE! YOU'RE ON CANDID CAMERA!

Many recent reports of paranormal activity involve so-called spirits captured on camera. Some claims involve security cameras. This was the case in 2014 at a New Mexico police station, whose security footage showed a ghostly figure walking across a room. According to the officer on duty, both doors to the room were locked and armed with an alarm, which never went off. Other reports involve images of spirits captured on smartphones. For example, in June 2014, an English tourist said she captured a photo using her iPhone of what appears to be a female ghost in period costume. Interestingly, although the figure was captured on camera, she was not visible to the naked eye. Of course, digital photos are easily doctored using simple computer software. Still, perhaps this type of photographic evidence will help future researchers settle the issue of the existence of ghosts once and for all.

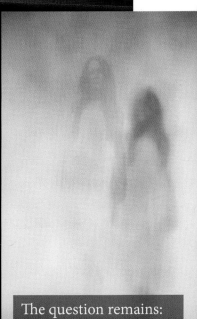

The question remains: Are ghosts real?

GLOSSARY

channel To allow a spirit to borrow one's body and use it to communicate by speaking, writing, drawing, or tapping.

debunk To expose something as being false.

demoniac A person who has been possessed by a demon.

exorcism A technique used by church officials to treat people who believe they are possessed. Someone who conducts an exorcism is called an exorcist.

hoax A deliberate attempt to pass off something false as being true.

medium Someone who acts as a bridge between the spirit world and the world of the living. Most mediums have been proven to be frauds.

occult Beliefs, practices, or phenomena that are supernatural, mystical, or magical in nature.

omen An event that is seen as a sign of events to come.

paranormal Describes events that cannot be explained by modern science.

parapsychology The study of the paranormal.

possession Describes when a demon, devil, or evil spirit takes control of a living person's body. Not to be confused with channeling.

pseudoscience Beliefs or practices that are thought to be scientific in nature, but in fact are not.

séance A gathering in which people attempt to contact the dead, usually with the help of a medium.

shamanic Describes an altered state of consciousness that enables one to interact with the spirit world.

skeptic A person who questions or doubts.

Spiritualism The belief that the dead live on in a spirit world and can communicate with the living with the help of a medium.

FURTHER INFORMATION

Books

Buell, Ryan, and Stefan Petrucha. *Paranormal State: My Journey into the Unknown.* New York: HarperCollins, 2010.

Clarke, Arthur C., and James Randi. *An Encyclopedia of Claims, Frauds, and Hoaxes of the Occult and Supernatural.* New York: St. Martins Press, 1995.

Clarke, Roger. *Ghosts: A Natural History of 500 Years of Searching for Proof.* New York: Macmillan, 2014.

Websites

Unexplained Mysteries
http://www.unexplained-mysteries.com
Catch up on the latest examples of unexplained happenings, including ghost sightings and demonic possessions.

Your Ghost Stories
http://www.yourghoststories.com
Scare yourself silly reading first-person accounts of ghost encounters.

Videos

Curious World: The Story of the Brown Lady of Raynham Hall
https://www.youtube.com/watch?v=GdJt6LRfXDk
This brief video gives the story of the Brown Lady of Raynham Hall and the famous photograph thought to be of her.

Ellen: Theresa Caputo Reads Ellen's Audience
https://www.youtube.com/watch?v=FPRCYgHEMdc
This video shows modern-day medium Theresa Caputo channeling deceased relatives of Ellen DeGeneres's audience.

Ghost Hunters
http://www.syfy.com/ghosthunters/videos
See episodes of the show *Ghost Hunters* from the Discovery Channel.

Paranormal State
http://www.aetv.com/shows/paranormal-state
Watch episodes of A&E's show *Paranormal State*, which explored various paranormal phenomena.

BIBLIOGRAPHY

Amorth, Father Gabriele. *An Exorcist Explains the Demonic: The Antics of Satan and His Army of Fallen.* Bedford, NH: Sophia Institute Press, 2016.

Carroll, Robert Todd. "Paranormal Investigator." Accessed December 1, 2016. http://skepdic.com/ paranormalinvestigator.html.

Cristiani, Leon. "Evidence of Satan in the Modern World." *Eternal World Television Network.* Accessed December 1, 2016. http://www.ewtn.com/library/ NEWAGE/EVIDSATN.htm.

Dickens, Charles. 1957. *Christmas Stories.* Oxford, UK: Oxford University Press.

Finucane, R.C. *Appearances of the Dead: A Cultural History of Ghosts.* New York: Prometheus Books, 1984.

Flanagin, Jake. "There Is a Paranormal Lab at the University of Virginia." February 10, 2014. Accessed December 1, 2016. http://www.theatlantic.com/health/archive/2014/02/ there-is-a-paranormal-activity-lab-at-the-university-of-virginia/283584.

Fodor, Nandor. "The Poltergeist, Psychoanalyzed." *The Psychiatric Quarterly* (1948): 195-203.

Guiley, Rosemary. *The Guinness Encyclopedia of Ghosts and Spirits.* London, UK: Guinness World Records Limited, 1994.

Hines, Terence. *Pseudoscience and the Paranormal.* New York: Prometheus Books, 2003.

Kurtz, Paul. *Skepticism and Humanism: The New Paradigm.* Livingston, NJ: Transaction Publisher, 2001.

Lewis, James R. *Satanism Today: An Encyclopedia of Religion, Folklore, and Popular Culture.* Santa Barbara, CA: ABC-CLIO, 2001.

Marryat, Florence. *There Is No Death.* New York: Lovell, Coryell & Co, 1891.

Martin, Malachi. *Hostage to the Devil.* San Francisco, CA: Harper, 1992.

Nickell, Joe. 2001. "Exorcism! Driving Out the Nonsense." *Skeptical Inquirer,* January/February 2001. Accessed December 1, 2016. http://www.csicop.org/si/show/exorcism_driving_out_the_nonsense.

Opsasnick, Mark. "The Haunted Boy of Cottage City." *Strange Magazine.* 1999.

Price, Harry. *Fifty Years of Psychical Research.* Whitefish, MT: Kessinger, 2003.

Radford, Benjamin. "The Shady Science of Ghost Hunting." October 27, 2006. Accessed December 1, 2016. http://www. livescience.com/4261-shady-science-ghost-hunting.html.

Radin, Dean. "Creative or Defective?" *Shift* magazine. 2005.

Rowe, Mike. "Paranormal Normal: Off the Wall." July 30, 2014. http://mikerowe.com/2014/07/paranormal-normal.

Sommer, Barbara A. "Participant Observation." Accessed December 1, 2016. http://psc.dss.ucdavis.edu/sommerb/sommerdemo/observation/partic.htm.

Winthrop, John, and James Kendall Hosmer. *Winthrop's Journal "History of New England" 1630-1649*. New York: Charles Scribner's Sons, 1908.

INDEX

Page numbers in **boldface** are illustrations. Entries in **boldface** are glossary terms.

ABOUT
THE AUTHOR

Kate Shoup has written more than forty books and has edited hundreds more. When not working, Shoup loves to watch IndyCar racing, ski, read, and ride her motorcycle. She lives in Indianapolis with her husband, her daughter, and their dog. To learn more about Kate and her work, visit http://www.kateshoup.com.